Speaking
In
Tongues

Clif Crosby II

Copyright © 2017 Clif Crosby II

All rights reserved.

Scripture quotations in this book are from the King James Version of the Bible unless otherwise identified.

Scriptures noted as English Standard Version are from The Holy Bible, English Standard Version, copyright © 2001 by Crossway Bibles, a division of Good News Publishers.

ISBN: 1544962088
ISBN-13: 978-1544962085

Speaking In Tongues

DEDICATION

I dedicate this book to every seeker of truth

"10. And the brethren immediately sent away Paul and Silas by night unto Berea: who coming thither went into the synagogue of the Jews.
11. These were more noble than those in Thessalonica, in that they received the word with all readiness of mind, and searched the scriptures daily, whether those things were so.
12. Therefore many of them believed; also of honourable women which were Greeks, and of men, not a few."
(Acts 17:10-12)

CONTENTS

ACKNOWLEDGMENTS

I want to thank everyone that assisted me in this project. If you helped and your name is not here please know that I appreciate all of your help.

Thanks to Pastor Peter Connell, Oakley, California and to Missionary R. Keith Nix, Peru, South America, for your help with this project. You men gave valuable input that is much appreciated.

Thanks to my lovely wife, Jennifer, for everything. You are the second best gift that God ever gave me.

Thanks to my wonderful kids, Cora, Molly and Quin for being supportive of my work.

Thanks to the Apostolic Saints at Union Pentecostal Church for having patience with me as I talk about, "my next book".

Thanks to the many men of God that have went before me that preached the glorious truth that is discussed in this booklet; including my deceased father, Pastor R. C. Crosby I.

Thanks to the only wise God, Jesus my Savior, for every good and every perfect gift.

PREFACE

In our present day, the practice of "speaking in tongues," called *glossolalia* by some authors, is a phenomenon and practice not clearly understood by many. Confusion may stem from religious traditions that have discounted speaking in tongues as being not-relevant to our modern day, or even confusion between what happened in Acts chapter two, when many were *"filled with the Holy Ghost, and began to speak with other tongues,"* and the *"gift of tongues"* mentioned in 1 Corinthians 12-14. These two phenomenons are not the same, although they have "speaking with other tongues" in common.

In this book, I intend to explain what is meant, Biblically, by the term "speaking in tongues," and to answer some of the questions regarding this practice, as well as common objections to the practice. It is imperative that every doctrine of the Church be based squarely and solely on a right dividing of the Word of truth, and not on the traditions of men, or upon poor exegesis of the Scriptures. Since the Old Testament is foundational to the New Testament, and is frequently quoted in the New Testament (and indeed constituted the "Scriptures" for the church in its infancy), we shall begin there.

CHAPTER 1

THE OLD TESTAMENT

"1. Woe to the crown of pride, to the drunkards of Ephraim, whose glorious beauty is a fading flower, which are on the head of the fat valleys of them that are overcome with wine!

2. Behold, the Lord hath a mighty and strong one, which as a tempest of hail and a destroying storm, as a flood of mighty waters overflowing, shall cast down to the earth with the hand.

3. The crown of pride, the drunkards of Ephraim, shall be trodden under feet:

4. And the glorious beauty, which is on the head of the fat valley, shall be a fading flower, and as the hasty fruit before the

summer; which when he that looketh upon it seeth, while it is yet in his hand he eateth it up.

5. In that day shall the LORD of hosts be for a crown of glory, and for a diadem of beauty, unto the residue of his people,

6. And for a spirit of judgment to him that sitteth in judgment, and for strength to them that turn the battle to the gate.

7. But they also have erred through wine, and through strong drink are out of the way; the priest and the prophet have erred through strong drink, they are swallowed up of wine, they are out of the way through strong drink; they err in vision, they stumble in judgment.

8. For all tables are full of vomit and filthiness, so that there is no place clean.

9. Whom shall he teach knowledge? and whom shall he make to understand doctrine? them that are weaned from the milk, and drawn from the breasts.

10. For precept must be upon precept, precept upon precept; line upon line, line upon line; here a little,and there a little:

11. For with stammering lips and another tongue will he speak to this people.

12. To whom he said, This is the rest wherewith ye may cause the weary to rest; and this is the refreshing: yet they would not hear.

13. But the word of the LORD was unto them precept upon precept, precept upon precept; line upon line, line upon line; here a little, and there a little; that they might go, and fall backward, and be broken, and snared, and taken."
(Isaiah 28:1-13)

The only Old Testament passage that directly addresses speaking in tongues is Isaiah 28:11. Isaiah 28 addresses *"the priest and the prophet"* who *"have erred."* The scripture says of these men that they are out of the way, err in vision and stumble in judgment. I would not want to follow anyone with any of these three conditions and especially not someone with all of these conditions.

"The priest and the prophet" had responded to the words of Isaiah with ridicule asking, *"Whom shall he teach knowledge? Whom shall he make to understand?"* then implying that the teaching was for children. They further mocked the teaching from the Lord by saying, *"precept must be upon precept, precept upon precept; line upon line, line upon line; here a little, and there a little."*

Isaiah replies, *"for with stammering lips and another tongue will He speak to this people,"* and regarding this, it was said that this was *"the rest wherewith ye may cause the weary to rest, and this is the refreshing."* We **know** that these scriptures refer, at least in the *sensus plenior* (the "fuller sense"), to the practice of "speaking with tongues." We **know** this because Paul in his discourse on tongues quotes Isaiah 28:11 and directly applies it to speaking in tongues in I Corinthians 14:21-22.

"21. In the law it is written, With men of other tongues and other lips will I speak unto this people; and yet for all that will they not hear me, saith the Lord.

22. Wherefore tongues are for a sign, not to them that believe, but to them that believe not: but prophesying serveth not for them that believe not, but for them which believe."

(I Corinthians 14:21-22)

CHAPTER 2

THE NEW TESTAMENT:

THE GOSPELS

There are four books that are called "the Gospels" in the New Testament: Matthew, Mark, Luke and John. Of these four, Mark is the only one to directly mentions "speaking in tongues".

"15. And he said unto them, Go ye into all the world, and preach the gospel to every creature.

16. He that believeth and is baptized shall be saved; but he that believeth not shall be damned.

17. And these signs shall follow them that believe; In my name shall they cast out devils; they shall speak with new tongues;

18. They shall take up serpents; and if they drink any deadly thing, it shall not hurt them; they shall lay hands on the sick, and they shall recover."

(Mark 16:15-18)

Mark states that signs shall follow believers. He lists several signs including *"they shall speak with new tongues."* This is a sign of a believer. A believer will speak with a tongue (language) that they have not learned. This point will be substantiated below.

Luke quotes Jesus saying, *"I send the promise of the Father upon you: but tarry in Jerusalem until ye be endued with power from on high"* (Luke 24:49). In his second book, The Acts of the Apostles, Luke again quotes Jesus, *"wait for the promise of the Father...ye shall be baptized with the Holy Ghost not many days hence"* (Acts 1:4,5) and, *"ye shall receive power after that the Holy Ghost is come upon you"* (Acts 1:8). As we shall see, when this happened the first time (Acts 2:4), it was accompanied by *"speaking in other tongues;"* and in subsequent times that people were filled with the Holy Ghost in the Scriptures, those who were present with them "**knew**" they had received the Holy Ghost because of the fact that they *"heard them speak with tongues."*

CHAPTER 3

THE NEW TESTAMENT:

ACTS

The Jews

In the second chapter of his history of the church Luke writes, *"And when the day of Pentecost was fully come, they were all with one accord in one place. And suddenly there came a sound from heaven as of a rushing mighty wind, and it filled all the house where they were sitting. And there appeared unto them cloven tongues like as of fire, and it sat upon each of them. And they were all filled with the Holy Ghost, and began to speak with other tongues as the Spirit gave them utterance"* (Acts 2:1-4).

Three things that should be pointed out here:

1. The Holy Ghost is the promise of the Father (Luke 24:49 and Acts 1:5,8).

2. The baptism of the Holy Ghost *caused them* to speak with tongues—it was *"as the Spirit gave them utterance"* (Acts 2:4).

3. They did not learn to speak with tongues, but the Holy Ghost (the Spirit) spoke (gave the utterance) through them (Acts 2:4).

This was a new experience! There is no record of men ever before speaking in a language that they had not learned, but these men and women did just that. The crowd that was at Jerusalem *"from every nation under heaven"* was confounded *"because that every man heard them speak in his own language"* (Acts 2:6). This amazed some and bewildered others! The hearers said, *"We do hear them speak in our tongues the wonderful works of God."* These people were excited about this "new thing". Peter preached to them in a language, Koine Greek, that they all knew and told them, *"This Jesus...having received of the Father the promise of the Holy Ghost...hath shed forth this, which ye now see and hear."* They heard them "speak with other tongues" and Peter applied this phenomenon of speaking with other tongues to *"the promise of the Father"*.

After hearing Peter's message many in the crowd were convicted of their sins—they felt the weight of their sins, and asked Peter and the rest of the Apostles, *"what shall we do?"* This is the same question that must be asked when we recognize that we have sinned. Peter's answer was direct. It was an answer that was overflowing with hope! Peter replied, *"Repent, and be baptized every one of you in the name of Jesus Christ for the remission of sins, and ye shall receive the gift of the Holy Ghost. For the promise* (remember, this was "the promise of the Father") *is unto you, and to your children, and to all that are afar off, even as many as the Lord our God shall call"* (Acts 2:38,39).

The promise of being *"filled with the Holy Ghost"* was to those who repented, and were baptized in the name of Jesus Christ for the remission of sins. In other words, the path to be assured of receiving the Holy Ghost is repentance from sins followed by immersion (in water) *"in the name of Jesus Christ."* The outpouring on the Day of Pentecost was limited to the Jews and Jewish proselytes, but Peter said in his message that day, *"whosoever shall call on the name of the Lord shall be saved."* This was a quote from Joel 2:32, and was a statement showing that salvation was not limited to the Jews only. It was not a statement telling the requirements for salvation. Peter went on to say, *"the promise is unto you, and to your children, and to all that are afar off, even as many as the Lord our God shall call."* Peter did not at this time believe that salvation, the "new birth" of John 3:3,5, was available for the Gentiles, but under the anointing of the Spirit of God he indeed stated that such was the case.

<u>The Gentiles</u>

In Acts, chapter 10 we find the Apostle Peter staying in Joppa at the house of a man named Simon. As was his custom Peter began to pray; and as he prayed he became very hungry. While he was waiting for his food to be prepared he was shown a vision by God. The ultimate fulfillment of the vision was the "new birth" of Gentiles.

Cornelius was a devout man, one that feared God, gave much alms, and prayed to God always, but **he still was not saved (Acts 11:14)**. God sent an angel to him in a vision stating, *"Thine prayers and thine alms are come up for a memorial before God...call for Peter...he shall tell thee what thou oughtest to do."* Peter's recounting of the events at Cornelius' house tells us plainly that the angel told him that Peter would *"tell thee words, whereby **thou** and all thy house **shall be saved**"* (Acts 11:14). The angel did not tell Cornelius how to be saved, but told him to hear the preacher. This goes with what Paul taught regarding salvation being in response to preaching (Romans 10:14-17).

When Peter arrived at Cornelius' house and started preaching his first words were, *"Of a truth I perceive that God is no respecter of persons."* As he continued to preach about "Jesus" he said, *"through his name whosoever believeth in him shall receive remission of sins."* While Peter was preaching the Holy Ghost fell upon the Gentiles. The Jews that were with Peter were astonished *"because that on the Gentiles also was poured out the gift of the Holy Ghost."* Now—for a very important question: How did they **know** that the Gentiles had received the Holy Ghost? Acts 10:46 plainly tells us the answer: *"For they heard them speak with tongues."*

The promise truly was to *"all that are afar off."* The promise truly was for *"whosoever shall call on the name of the Lord."* The Gentiles also received the Holy Ghost. The way that the Jews knew that the Gentiles had received the Holy Ghost was, *"For they heard them speak with tongues, and magnify God."* Peter then said that the Gentiles had *"received the Holy Ghost"* as well as the Jews had (Acts 10:47). In another place Peter said, *"the Holy Ghost fell on them, as on us at the beginning"* (Acts 11:15-17). Then Peter commanded them to be baptized in the name of the Lord.

This was the outpouring of the Holy Ghost to the Gentiles, and just like the outpouring to the Jews it was evidenced by *"speaking in tongues"* and occurred in conjunction with Jesus' name baptism (albeit in reverse order), for the context tells us that Peter would have been unlikely to immerse them in Jesus' name had the Gentiles not received the Holy Ghost, evidenced by *"speaking in other tongues"*, first. Jesus in John 3:3,5 said that no one could see nor enter the kingdom of God without being born (again) of the water and of the Spirit. The New Birth of water is water baptism (immersion) in having the name of Jesus invoked over the one being baptized (this is clearly how the early church understood Jesus' words). The New Birth of the Spirit is the baptism of the Holy Ghost with speaking in tongues as the Spirit gives the utterance. As we look into the teaching of the Apostles in their letters to the church a little later, we shall see that they understood and stated that salvation was wrought in believers' lives, *"not by works of righteousness…, but according to his mercy…BY the washing of regeneration* [washing of re-birth], *and renewing of the Holy Ghost* [being made new through the Holy Ghost]" (Titus 3:5).

The Believers

In Acts 19 we see that the Apostle Paul traveled to Ephesus, and there he found disciples. They were believers, having followed the teaching of John the Baptist who prepared the way before Jesus Christ. Paul asked them, *"Have you received the Holy Ghost since ye believed?"* They replied, *"We have not so much as heard whether there be any Holy Ghost."* One translation says, *"Nay, we did not so much as hear whether the Holy Spirit was given."* [Acts 19:2. American Standard Version. Public Domain.] They were believers, but they had not been born again according to John 3:3,5 and Acts 2:38. Paul's next question verifies this. Paul gets right to the point, and asks a question that we would all do well to ask ourselves as well. He asks, *"Unto what then were you baptized?"* They answered that they had been baptized unto John's baptism. John was a good man with a good message, but his message had been superseded.

John preached repentance and baptism with *"the baptism of repentance"*, but he also preached that One would come after who was greater than he, and that He would come with a "better baptism." **John's message was good, but it was not everlasting. More was required than what John preached.** After Paul explained this to them, *"they were baptized in the name of the Lord Jesus,"* thus fulfilling Mark 16:16 and part of John 3:3,5 and Acts 2:38. Paul then laid his hands upon them and the Holy Ghost came upon them. When the Holy Ghost came we see that familiar evidence again that we had seen in Acts 2 and in Acts 10, *"they spoke with tongues…."*

Thus far we have seen that when the Jews, the Gentiles, and the religious believers received the Holy Ghost they *"spoke in tongues."* We have also seen baptism performed and/or commanded in *"the name of Jesus"* in each of these cases.

If you have not been filled with the Holy Ghost, evidenced by speaking in tongues, then you have not received the promise of the Father. If you have not repented and been baptized (immersed in water) having the name of Jesus invoked over you, you have not received remission of sins. **Yet these experiences are for you!**.

CHAPTER 4

THE NEW TESTAMENT:

LETTERS TO THE CHURCHES

Paul, in his first letter to the church at Corinth, also addresses speaking in tongues. Chapters 12-14 of I Corinthians give us additional insight to this practice. All of the references in the book of Acts deal with people speaking in tongues when they are first filled with the Holy Ghost and are baptized in water in the name of Jesus, thus being born again. It appears there as **the confirmatory sign** that they had received the

Holy Ghost, *"for they heard them speak with tongues"* (Acts 10:46). In I Corinthians, the Apostle Paul shows us **another facet** of speaking in tongues. The book of I Corinthians is written **to the church** so **it is written to people that had already experienced speaking in tongues when they were saved** (Mark 16:15-18; John 3:3,5; Acts 2:4,38; 10:44-47; 19:1-7)

Chapter 12 introduces us to this new facet. We read about nine separate *"gifts of the Spirit."* Two of these are *"divers kinds of tongues"* and *"the interpretation of tongues"*. These gifts are not to be confused with the tongue that accompanies the baptism (infilling) of the Holy Ghost as seen at the conversion of people in the book of Acts. These gifts are *"given to every man to profit withal."* These gifts "are in the church", yet not everyone experiences each particular gift. Paul asked regarding the gift of tongues *"do all speak with tongues?"* He was not asking this regarding the *"speaking with tongues"* that accompanies *"the baptism of the Holy Ghost"*—which appears in Acts to be the single consistent sign that someone received the Holy Ghost—but the gift of *"diverse kinds of tongues"* that he introduced in this chapter.

Chapter 13 shows that the gift of tongues, not motivated by love, is just noise. Paul goes on to tell us that it and other gifts are simply based on knowledge *"in part"* and that they are needed until *"that which is perfect is come,"* at which time, *"that which is in part* [including tongues] *shall be done away."* Contextually, this clearly speaks of the time that Christ returns for His church, and our knowledge and understanding are "complete" (which is the meaning of the Greek word, *teleios*, translated as "perfect").

Chapter 14 goes into much detail concerning tongues and prophecy. Both of these subjects are regarding the gift mentioned in Chapter 12.

Let's look at the following:

"He that speaketh in an unknown tongue speaketh not unto men, but unto God:..." (I Corinthians 14:2)

Man does not understand this tongue, but God does.

In the Spirit the *"tongue talker"* is speaking mysteries. Again, these tongues are not the *"speaking in tongues"* that accompany *"the baptism of the Holy Ghost."* It is the spiritual gift of I Corinthians 12:10 given to some of those who have already been born again. It refers to *"divers kinds of tongues"* which is either intended for *"interpretation of tongues"* or for private devotion (prayer) wherein the speaker is edified alone.

"He that speaketh in an unknown tongues edifies (builds up) *himself;..."* (I Corinthians 14:4)

Jude refers to this when he says, *"But ye, beloved, building up yourselves on your most holy faith, praying in the Holy Ghost."* [Jude 1:20 King James Version] This *"praying in the Holy Ghost"* includes speaking in tongues. When you *"speak in tongues"*, you are building yourself up, building your spiritual strength, much like when a runner builds his strength for a race by exercise.

"I want you all to speak in tongues..." (I Corinthians 14:5 English Standard Version)

Paul seems to be saying, "Don't take this as teaching against speaking in tongues. I want you to speak in tongues regularly."

"...If I pray in an unknown tongue, my spirit prayeth..." (I Corinthians 14:14).

This may also be referenced by Paul in Romans 8.

"26. Likewise the Spirit also helpeth our infirmities: for we know not what we should pray for as we ought: but the Spirit itself maketh intercession for us with groanings which cannot be uttered.
27. And he that searcheth the hearts knoweth what is the mind of the Spirit, because he maketh intercession for the saints according to the will of God." (Romans 8:26-27)

"...I will pray with the spirit, ...I will sing with the spirit,..." (I Corinthians 14:15)

Here again Paul is encouraging speaking in tongues, for it is obvious that he is contrasting praying or singing *"with the spirit"* and praying or singing in his **known** language.

"I thank my God, I speak with tongues more than ye all:" (I Corinthians 14:18).

Speaking in tongues should not be just limited to when one is saved from sin, but should be a continual experience in the life of the believer.

Tongues are for a sign to the unbeliever.

This point is made in I Corinthians 14:21-22. *"...tongues are for a sign, not to them that believe, but to them that believe not."* Verse 21 quotes Isaiah 28:11. **Just as tongues are a sign of the believer (Mark 16:17) they are a sign to the unbeliever**. The unbeliever will see the presence of God by the sign of tongues.

I Corinthians 14:27-28 gives rules for the use of the gifts.

These rules do not speak to the use of tongues when one is saved (See comments on the book of Acts), but to the use of the gifts of tongues after one is saved.

"...Forbid not to speak with tongues." (I Corinthians 14:39)

Paul concludes these chapters on the gift of tongues by saying, *"Forbid not to speak with tongues!"* When someone is "born again" they will speak with tongues and these tongues should not be *"forbidden"*, nor should *"the gift of tongues"* that is mentioned in I Corinthians 12-14 be forbidden.

CHAPTER 5

ANSWERING QUESTIONS

AND OBJECTIONS

Objections

1. Tongues are a gift to help missionaries carry the gospel to others.

The initial sign of tongues in Acts 2 does state that the men heard them speaking every man in his language, but the "tongue talking" did not preach the salvation message to them. Peter preached to them the message of the church in the language that they all understood, Koine Greek (common Greek), which was the *lingua franca* for most of the Roman Empire in that day. His message concluded with Acts 2:38-40, and their response to Peter's preaching of the gospel. Furthermore there is no reference in the book of Acts, the history of the church, that shows that missionaries "preached in tongues" nor "understood what natives spake in their native languages." Therefore, this objection is not valid.

2. *Tongues have ceased.*

Those who hold this view attempt to do so by referring to I Corinthians 13:8, but this verse will not be fulfilled until *"that which is perfect is come"* which is the making "complete" (Greek.: teleios – see comment on this in Chapter 5) of our experience upon the return of Jesus Christ. This is when *"tongues will cease,"* because *"that which is in part shall be done away."* The context of the passage makes this abundantly clear. Some attempt to say that the completion of our Bible was the *"that which is perfect"* referenced, and that tongues are not for us today—yet this argument cannot answer an important question: Has knowledge vanished away? The very same verse says that when that which is perfect will come that knowledge shall have vanished away. It is evident that to make this verse say that *"tongues have ceased"* for our day is to take the passage entirely out of its context. It is speaking of those things which are *"in part"*— whether it is tongues, prophecies or knowledge (speaking of the gifts) ceasing. That is, the 'in part' portion will cease when that which is perfect (complete) is come—and this will happen when we make heaven our home and there is no more need for that which is *"in part"* (the gifts). This passage actually supports the fact that the gifts will continue until He returns for His church.

3. Tongues are not essential to salvation.

Jesus said that we must be born again (John 3:3), which He identified as being born of water and of the Spirit (John 3:5). Tongues are identified as the universal Scriptural evidence showing that someone has been filled with the Spirit (Acts 2:4; 10:45-46; 19:6). It was the consistent evidence in all of these passages cited. In Acts 10, it is clear that the way those who accompanied Peter into the household of the Gentile, Cornelius, knew that they had received the Holy Ghost was because they heard them speak in tongues: *"While Peter yet spake these words, the Holy Ghost fell on all them which heard the word. And they of the circumcision which believed were astonished, as many as came with Peter, because that on the Gentiles also was poured out the gift of the Holy Ghost. For they heard them speak with tongues, and magnify God..."* (Acts 10:44-46). It was then, when Peter saw that they had received the gift of the Holy Ghost, that he commanded them to be immersed in the name of the Lord to fulfill their born-again experience. It is not that "tongues" are essential to salvation—it is that **the baptism of the Holy Ghost is essential to salvation. Tongues merely accompany—and give evidence of—that gift**.

4. Tongues are not mentioned in Acts 8 when Samaritans received the Holy Ghost—and someone receives the Holy Ghost when they just "believe."

I'm glad you brought that up! If you will notice, when Phillip went to the city of Samaria and *"preached Christ unto them"* (verse 5), he preached *"the things concerning the kingdom of God, and the name of Jesus Christ"* (verse 12) and he baptized them. During this time, *"they gave heed to those things which Phillip spake."* There were miracles, demons exorcised, great joy in the city, and many who were healed. The narrative also tells us that *"when they believed Phillip preaching the things concerning the kingdom of God, and the name of Jesus Christ, they were baptized, both men and women"* (Acts 8:12). Even with all of these things, they knew that these Samaritan people had not received the Holy Ghost (verses 14-16). Therefore Peter and John came from Jerusalem and laid hands on them that they might receive the Holy Ghost.

The question **MUST** be asked, *"How did they know that these people have not received the Holy Ghost?"* They knew that these folks had believed. They had been baptized. They had miraculous healings among them—yet they had NOT received the Holy Ghost. There must have been some conspicuous evidence that was missing.

When Peter and John laid hands on them, they received the Holy Ghost (Acts 8:17). When this happened, Simon the sorcerer **SAW** them receive the Holy Ghost and offered money that he could have power to make that happen by laying hands on people. Of course, he could not purchase the gift of God with money, Peter said—but the fact remains that:

* These people had both believed and were baptized <u>but had not received the Holy Ghost</u> when they believed.

* Phillip and the Apostles knew that they had not received the Holy Ghost, so there must have been some lack of an expected evidence.

* When the Apostles laid hands on them, they received the Holy Ghost, and a bystander (Simon)

saw (Greek: *eidō*, perceived with the senses) some sudden, conspicuous evidence that they had received the Holy Ghost. But, what was that sudden and conspicuous evidence? The **only** evidence that was uniformly noted as being the evidence of someone receiving the Holy Ghost throughout the book of Acts (Acts 2:4, 10:46, 19:6) was that they *"spoke with other tongues"*.

Questions

1. I love the Lord; why have I not spoke in tongues?

Cornelius loved the Lord, and the 12 at Ephesus loved the Lord, but they needed a preacher to tell them about the Holy Ghost and Jesus' name baptism. Look at the life of Cornelius before his conversion in Acts 10:2:

* A devout (reverent, godly) man

* Feared God

* Led his household in the fear of God

* Gave much alms to the poor

* Prayed continually to God

Yet Cornelius needed more—AND he was open to more. That is why the Lord sent him to call for a preacher of the gospel.

Have you heard about the Holy Ghost? Have you been baptized in Jesus' name? **If you will repent, and be baptized in the name of Jesus Christ for the remission of sins, you shall receive the gift of the Holy Ghost—speaking in other tongues as the Spirit gives the utterance** (Acts 2:38-39).

2. I don't know how to speak in tongues.

Good! Speaking in tongues is not learned! It happens when one is filled with the Holy Ghost.

CHAPTER 6

CONCLUSION

This experience of speaking in tongues as the Spirit of God gave the utterance was the normative experience of every convert noted in the book of the Acts of the Apostles. Receiving the Holy Ghost was and is part of the new birth experience that was never rescinded—and it was always evidenced (and still is) by speaking in other tongues as the Spirit of God gives the utterance.

The gift of *"divers kinds of tongues"* continues as a normative and useful gift in the church, along with the other eight spiritual gifts, until the time that the Lord Jesus returns for His church.

If you (the reader) have not yet received the gift of the Holy Ghost, evidenced by speaking in other tongues, this promise extends to you today. By repenting truly of your sins and following in obedience to the gospel message by being baptized (immersed in water) in Jesus name (having His name invoked over you)—which was the consistent message and experience in the days of the Apostles—you have the promise that you will be filled with the Holy Ghost! What an opportunity awaits the sincere seeker of Truth. May God bless you as you search the Scriptures and avail yourself of this greatest of gifts.

Books by Clif Crosby II

* The Jesus Name Pentecostals of Neshoba County, Mississippi
* Speaking In Tongues

Coming Soon:
* The Jesus Name Pentecostals of Leake County, Mississippi

To purchase books you can contact the author via email at clifcrosby2@bellsouth.net

ABOUT THE AUTHOR

Clif Crosby II is the Pastor of Union Pentecostal Church in Union, Mississippi. He is the husband of the lovely Jennifer Crosby and the father of three wonderful children: Coralyn, Molly and Quinton. Speaking in Tongues is his second book

44585930R00029

Made in the USA
Middletown, DE
11 June 2017